IS-200.a - ICS for Single Resources and Initial Action Incidents

By FEMA

Based on Public Domain Text

Lesson Overview

The **Welcome/Course Overview** lesson reviews the Incident Command System features.

Incident Command System (ICS)

The Incident Command System (ICS):

- Is a standardized management tool for meeting the demands of small or large emergency or nonemergency situations.

- Represents "best practices," and has become the standard for emergency management across the country.

- May be used for planned events, natural disasters, and acts of terrorism.

- Is a key feature of the National Incident Management System (NIMS).

ICS is not just a standardized organizational chart, but an entire management system.

Why ICS?

All levels of government, the private sector, and non-governmental agencies must be prepared to prevent, protect against, respond to, and recover from a wide spectrum of major events and natural disasters that exceed the capabilities of any single entity. Threats from natural disasters and human-caused events, such as terrorism, require a unified and coordinated national approach to planning and to domestic incident management.

Homeland Security Presidential Directives

To address this need, President Bush issued the following Homeland Security Presidential Directives (HSPDs):

- HSPD-5 identifies steps for improved coordination in response to incidents. It requires the Department of Homeland Security (DHS) to coordinate with other Federal departments and agencies and State, local, and tribal governments to establish a National Incident Management System (NIMS).

- HSPD-8 describes the way Federal departments and agencies will prepare. It requires DHS to coordinate with other Federal departments and agencies and State, local, and tribal governments to develop national preparedness guidelines.

National Incident Management System (NIMS)

NIMS provides a consistent framework for incident management at all jurisdictional levels regardless of the cause, size, or complexity of the incident. Building upon the Incident Command System (ICS), the NIMS provides the Nation's first responders and authorities with the same foundation for incident management for terrorist attacks, natural disasters, and other emergencies. NIMS requires that ICS be institutionalized.

NIMS Components

NIMS integrates existing best practices into a consistent, nationwide approach to domestic incident management. Five major components make up the NIMS systems approach:

- Command and Management

- Preparedness

- Resource Management

- Communications and Information Management

- Ongoing Management and Maintenance

The Incident Command System, Multiagency Coordination Systems, and Public Information all fall under Command and Management.

ICS Features

ICS is based on proven management principles, which contribute to the strength and efficiency of the overall system.

ICS principles are implemented through a wide range of management features including the use of common terminology and clear text, and a modular organizational structure.

ICS emphasizes effective planning, including management by objectives and reliance on an Incident Action Plan.

ICS helps ensure full utilization of all incident resources by:

- Maintaining a manageable span of control.

- Establishing predesignated incident locations and facilities.

- Implementing resource management practices.

- Ensuring integrated communications.

The ICS features related to command structure include chain of command and unity of command as well as unified command and transfer of command. Formal transfer of command occurs whenever leadership changes.

Through accountability and mobilization, ICS helps ensure that resources are on hand and ready.

And, finally ICS supports responders and decisionmakers by providing the data they need through effective information and intelligence management.

ICS Features

This course builds on what you learned in ICS-100 about ICS features. The ICS features are listed below.

- Common Terminology

- Modular Organization

- Management by Objectives

- Reliance on an Incident Action Plan (IAP)

- Chain of Command and Unity of Command

- Unified Command

- Manageable Span of Control

- Predesignated Incident Locations and Facilities

- Resource Management

- Information and Intelligence Management

- Integrated Communications

- Transfer of Command

- Accountability

- Mobilization

Common Terminology. Using common terminology helps to define organizational functions, incident facilities, resource descriptions, and position titles.

Modular Organization. The incident command organizational structure develops in a top-down, modular fashion that is based on the size and complexity of the incident, as well as the specifics of the hazard environment created by the incident.

Management by Objectives. Includes establishing overarching objectives; developing and issuing assignments, plans, procedures, and protocols; establishing specific, measurable objectives for various incident management functional activities; and directing efforts to attain the established objectives.

Reliance on an Incident Action Plan. Incident Action Plans (IAPs) provide a coherent means of communicating the overall incident objectives in the contexts of both operational and support activities.

Chain of Command and Unity of Command. Chain of command refers to the orderly line of authority within the ranks of the incident management organization. Unity of command means that every individual has a designated supervisor to whom he or she reports at the scene of the incident. These principles clarify reporting relationships and eliminate the confusion caused by multiple, conflicting directives. Incident managers at all levels must be able to control the actions of all personnel under their supervision.

Unified Command. In incidents involving multiple jurisdictions, a single jurisdiction with multiagency involvement, or multiple jurisdictions with multiagency involvement, Unified Command allows agencies with different legal, geographic, and functional authorities and responsibilities to work together effectively without affecting individual agency authority, responsibility, or accountability.

Manageable Span of Control. Span of control is key to effective and efficient incident management. Within ICS, the span of control of any individual with incident management supervisory responsibility should range from three to seven subordinates.

Predesignated Incident Locations and Facilities. Various types of operational locations and support facilities are established in the vicinity of an incident to accomplish a variety of purposes. Typical predesignated facilities include Incident Command Posts, Bases, Camps, Staging Areas, Helibases, and Helispots. Additional facilities such as Mass Casualty Triage Areas and others may be added as required.

Resource Management. Resource management includes processes for categorizing, ordering, dispatching, tracking, and recovering resources. It also includes processes for reimbursement for resources, as appropriate. Resources are defined as personnel, teams, equipment, supplies, and facilities available or potentially available for assignment or allocation in support of incident management and emergency response activities.

Information and Intelligence Management. The incident management organization must establish a process for gathering, sharing, and managing incident-related information and intelligence.

Integrated Communications. Incident communications are facilitated through the development and use of a common communications plan and interoperable communications processes and architectures.

Transfer of Command. The command function must be clearly established from the beginning of an incident. When command is transferred, the process must include a briefing that captures all essential information for continuing safe and effective operations.

Accountability. Effective accountability at all jurisdictional levels and within individual functional areas during incident operations is essential. To that end, the following principles must be adhered to:

- **Check-In.** All responders, regardless of agency affiliation, must report in to receive an assignment in accordance with the procedures established by the Incident Commander.

- **Incident Action Plan.** Response operations must be directed and coordinated as outlined in the IAP.

- **Unity of Command.** Each individual involved in incident operations will be assigned to only one supervisor.

- **Span of Control.** Supervisors must be able to adequately supervise and control their subordinates, as well as communicate with and manage all resources under their supervision.

- **Resource Tracking.** Supervisors must record and report resource status changes as they occur.

Mobilization. Personnel and equipment should respond only when requested or when dispatched by an appropriate authority.

Lesson 2: Leadership and Management

Lesson Overview

The **Leadership and Management** lesson provides a more detailed look at the following ICS features:

- Chain of Command and Unity of Command

- Span of Control

- Leadership in Incident Management

- Common Terminology

At the end of this lesson, you should be able to:

- Describe chain of command and formal communication relationships.

- Identify common leadership responsibilities.

- Describe span of control and modular development.

- Describe the use of position titles.

Unity of Command

Unity of command means that each individual involved in incident operations will be assigned to only one supervisor to whom they report.

Chain of command and unity of command help to ensure that clear reporting relationships exist and eliminate the confusion caused by multiple, conflicting directives. Incident managers at all levels must be able to control the actions of all personnel under their supervision.

Unity of command clears up many of the potential communication problems encountered in managing incidents or events by maintaining formal communication relationship only with one's immediate supervisor.

Don't confuse **unity** of command with **Unified** Command!

Unified Command

Responsible agencies manage an incident together under a **Unified Command**.

Unified Command:

- Enables all responsible agencies to manage an incident together by establishing a common set of incident objectives and strategies.

- Allows Incident Commanders to make joint decisions by establishing a single command structure at one Incident Command Post (ICP).

- Maintains unity of command. Each employee only reports to one supervisor.

Advantages of Unified Command

Advantages of using Unified Command include:

- A single set of objectives guides incident response.

- A collective approach is used to develop strategies to achieve incident objectives.

- Information flow and coordination are improved between all involved in the incident.

- All agencies have an understanding of joint priorities and restrictions.

- No agency's legal authorities will be compromised or neglected.

- Agencies' efforts are optimized as they perform their respective assignments under a single Incident Action Plan.

Formal Communication

Formal communication must be used when:

- Receiving and giving work assignments.

- Requesting support or additional resources.

- Reporting progress of assigned tasks.

Other information concerning the incident or event can be passed horizontally or vertically within the organization without restriction. This is known as **informal** communication.

Informal Communication

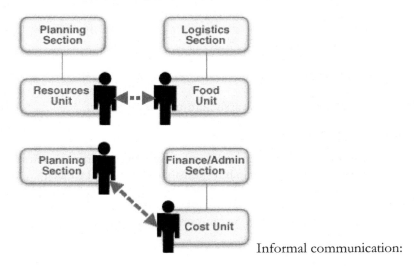

Informal communication:

- Is used to exchange incident or event information only.

- Is **NOT** used for:

  o Formal requests for additional resources.

  o Tasking work assignments.

Examples of informal communication are as follows:

- The Food Unit Leader may directly contact the Resources Unit Leader to determine the number of persons requiring feeding.

- The Cost Unit Leader may directly discuss and share information on alternative strategies with the Planning Section Chief.

Incident Leadership

As a leader during an incident, you must provide purpose, direction, and motivation for responders who are working to accomplish difficult tasks under dangerous, stressful circumstances.

Leadership

Leadership means providing purpose, direction, and motivation for responders working to accomplish difficult tasks under dangerous, stressful circumstances.

Common Leadership Responsibilities

A good leader:

- **ENSURES** safe work practices.

- **TAKES COMMAND** of assigned resources.

- **MOTIVATES** with a "can do safely" attitude.

- **DEMONSTRATES INITIATIVE** by taking action.

The safety of all personnel involved in an incident or a planned event is the **first duty of ICS leadership**. This is the overall responsibility of Team Leaders, Group or Division Supervisors, Branch Directors, Sections Chiefs, and all members of the Command or Unified Command staff. Ensuring safe work practices is the top priority within the ICS common leadership responsibilities.

In addition, a good leader:

- **COMMUNICATES** by giving specific instructions and asking for feedback.

- **SUPERVISES** the scene of action.

- **EVALUATES** the effectiveness of the plan.

- **UNDERSTANDS** and **ACCEPTS** the need to modify plans or instructions.

Leadership & Duty

Leaders should know, understand, and practice the leadership principles. Leaders need to recognize the relationship between these principles and the leadership values.

Duty is how you value your job. Duty begins with everything required of you by law and policy, but it is much more than simply fulfilling requirements. A leader commits to excellence in all aspects of his or her professional responsibility.

Commitment to Duty

What can you do, personally, that demonstrates your commitment to duty to those you lead?

As a leader, you should try to:

- Take charge within your scope of authority.

- Be prepared to step out of a tactical role to assume a leadership role.

- Be proficient in your job.

- Make sound and timely decisions.

- Ensure tasks are understood.

- Develop your subordinates for the future.

Leadership & Respect

In order to maintain leadership and respect, you should:

- **Know your subordinates and look out for their well-being.** The workers who follow you are your greatest resource. Not all of your workers will succeed equally, but they all deserve respect.

- **Keep your subordinates and supervisor informed.** Provide accurate and timely briefings, and give the reason (intent) for assignments and tasks.

- **Build the team.** Conduct frequent briefings and debriefings with the team to monitor progress and identify lessons learned. Consider team experience, fatigue, and physical limitations when accepting assignments.

Communication Responsibilities

To ensure sharing of critical information, all responders must:

- Brief others as needed.

- Debrief their actions.

- Communicate hazards to others.

- Acknowledge messages.

- Ask if they do not know.

While not always possible, the most effective form of communication is face-to-face.

Briefing Elements

Provide complete briefings that include clearly stated objectives and the following elements:

- Task: What is to be done.

- Purpose: Why it is to be done.

- End State: How it should look when done.

Incident Management Assessment

Assessment is an important leadership responsibility, and is conducted after a major activity in order to allow employees and leaders to discover what happened and why. Assessment methods include:

- Corrective action report/After-action review (AAR).

- Post-incident analysis (PIA).

- Debriefing.

- Post-incident critique.

- Mitigation plans.

Using Common Terminology

ICS establishes common terminology that allows diverse incident management and support entities to work together.

Major functions and functional units with incident management responsibilities are named and defined. Terminology for the organizational elements involved is standard and consistent.

ICS Organization: Review

The ICS organization:

- Is typically structured to facilitate activities in five major functional areas: command, operations, planning, logistics, and finance and administration.

- Is adaptable to any emergency or incident to which domestic incident management agencies would be expected to respond.

- Has a scalable organizational structure that is based on the size and complexity of the incident.

However, this flexibility does NOT allow for the modification of the standard, common language used to refer to organizational components or positions.

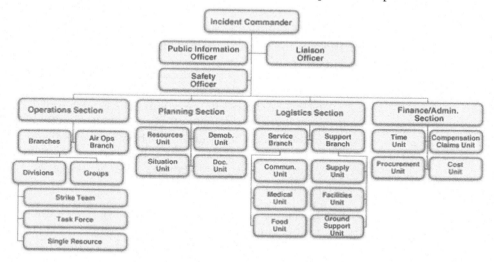

- **Incident Commander:** The individual responsible for all incident activities, including the development of strategies and tactics and the ordering and the release of resources. The IC has overall authority and responsibility for conducting incident operations and is responsible for the management of all incident operations at the incident site.

- **Command Staff:** The Command Staff consists of:

    o **Liaison Officer:** A member of the Command Staff responsible for coordinating with representatives from cooperating and assisting agencies. The Liaison Officer may have Assistants.

    o **Public Information Officer:** A member of the Command Staff responsible for interfacing with the public and media or with other agencies with incident-related information requirements.

    o **Safety Officer:** A member of the Command Staff responsible for monitoring and assessing safety hazards or unsafe situations, and for developing measures for ensuring personnel safety. The Safety Officer may have Assistants.

- **General Staff :** The organization level having functional responsibility for primary segments of incident management (Operations, Planning, Logistics, Finance/Administration). The Section level is organizationally between Branch and Incident Commander. Sections are as follows:

  - **Operations Section:** The Section responsible for all tactical operations at the incident and includes:

    - **Branch:** That organizational level having functional, geographical, or jurisdictional responsibility for major parts of the incident operations. The Branch level is organizationally between Section and Division/Group in the Operations Section, and between Section and Units in the Logistics Section. Branches are identified by the use of Roman Numerals, by function, or jurisdictional name.

    - **Division:** That organization level having responsibility for operations within a defined geographic area. The Division level is organizationally between the Strike Team and the Branch.

    - **Group:** Groups are established to divide the incident into functional areas of operation. Groups are located between Branches (when activated) and Resources in the Operations Section.

    - **Unit:** That organization element having functional responsibility for a specific incident planning, logistics, or finance activity.

    - **Task Force:** A group of resources with common communications and a leader that may be pre-established and sent to an incident, or formed at an incident.

    - **Strike Team:** Specified combinations of the same kind and type of resources, with common communications and a leader.

    - **Single Resources:** An individual piece of equipment and its personnel complement, or an established crew or team of individuals with an identified work supervisor, that can be used on an incident.

- o **Planning Section:** Responsible for the collection, evaluation, and dissemination of information related to the incident, and for the preparation and documentation of the Incident Action Plan. The Section also maintains information on the current and forecasted situation, and on the status of resources assigned to the incident. Includes the Situation, Resources, Documentation, and Demobilization Units, as well as Technical Specialists.

- o **Logistics Section:** The Section responsible for providing facilities, services, and materials for the incident. The Logistics Section includes the Service Branch (Communication Unit, Medical Unit, and Food Unit) and Support Branch (Supply Unit, Facilities Unit, and Ground Support Unit).

- o **Finance/Administration Section:** The Section responsible for all incident costs and financial considerations. Includes the Time Unit, Procurement Unit, Compensation/Claims Unit, and Cost Unit.

ICS Management: Span of Control

ICS span of control for any supervisor is between 3 and 7 subordinates, and optimally does not exceed 5 subordinates.

Modular Organization

The ICS organization adheres to a "form follows function" philosophy. The size of the current organization and that of the next operational period is determined through the incident planning process.

Because the ICS is a modular concept, managing span of control is accomplished by organizing resources into Teams, Divisions, Groups, Branches, or Sections when the supervisor-to-subordinate ratio exceeds 7, or by reorganizing or demobilizing Sections, Branches, Divisions, Groups, or Teams when the ratio falls below 3.

Typical Organizational Structure

The initial response to most domestic incidents is typically handled by local "911" dispatch centers, emergency responders within a single jurisdiction, and direct supporters of emergency responders. Most responses need go no further.

Approximately 95% of all incidents are small responses that include:

- • **Command:** Incident Commander and other Command Staff.

- **Single Resources:** An individual piece of equipment and its personnel complement, or an established crew or team of individuals with an identified work supervisor that can be used on an incident.

Expanding Incidents

Incidents that begin with single resources may rapidly expand requiring significant additional resources and operational support.

Use of Position Titles

At each level within the ICS organization, individuals with primary responsibility positions have distinct titles. Using specific ICS position titles serves these important purposes:

- Provides a common standard.

- Ensures qualified individuals fill positions.

- Ensures that requested personnel are qualified.

- Standardizes communication.

- Describes the responsibilities of the position.

ICS Supervisory Position Titles

Titles for all ICS supervisory levels are shown in the table below:

Organizational Level	Title	Support Position
Incident Command	Incident Commander	Deputy
Command Staff	Officer	Assistant
General Staff (Section)	Chief	Deputy
Branch	Director	Deputy
Division/Group	Supervisor	N/A
Unit	Leader	Manager
Strike Team/Task Force	Leader	Single Resource Boss

Lesson 3: Delegation of Authority & Management by Objectives

Lesson Overview

The **Delegation of Authority & Management by Objectives** lesson introduces you to the delegation of authority process, implementing authorities, management by objectives, and preparedness plans and objectives.

This lesson will:

- Describe the delegation of authority process.

- Describe scope of authority.

- Describe management by objectives.

- Describe the importance of preparedness plans and agreements.

Delegation of Authority Process

Authority is **a right or obligation to act** on behalf of a department, agency, or jurisdiction.

- In most jurisdictions, the responsibility for the protection of the citizens rests with the chief elected official. Elected officials have the authority to make decisions, commit resources, obligate funds, and command the resources necessary to protect the population, stop the spread of damage, and protect the environment.

- In private industry, this same responsibility and authority rests with the chief executive officer.

Scope of Authority

An Incident Commander's scope of authority is derived:

- From existing laws, agency policies, and procedures, and/or

- Through a delegation of authority from the agency administrator or elected official.

Delegation of Authority

The process of granting authority to carry out specific functions is called the **delegation of authority**.

Delegation of authority:

- Grants authority to carry out specific functions.

- Is issued by the chief elected official, chief executive officer, or agency administrator in writing or verbally.

- Allows the Incident Commander to assume command.

- Does **NOT** relieve the granting authority of the ultimate responsibility for the incident.

Ideally, this authority will be granted in writing. Whether it is granted in writing or verbally, the authorities granted remain with the Incident Commander until such time as the incident is terminated, or a relief shift Incident Commander is appointed, or the Incident Commander is relieved of his or her duties for just cause.

Delegation of Authority: When Not Needed

A delegation of authority may not be required if the Incident Commander is acting within his or her existing authorities.

An emergency manager may already have the authority to deploy response resources to a small flash flood.

A fire chief probably has the authority (as part of the job description) to serve as an Incident Commander at a structure fire.

Delegation of Authority: When Needed

A delegation of authority is needed:

- If the incident is outside the Incident Commander's home jurisdiction.

- When the incident scope is complex or beyond existing authorities.

- If required by law or procedures.

Delegation of Authority: Elements

When issued, delegation of authority should include:

- Legal authorities and restrictions.

- Financial authorities and restrictions.

- Reporting requirements.

- Demographic issues.

- Political implications.

- Agency or jurisdictional priorities.

- Plan for public information management.

- Process for communications.

- Plan for ongoing incident evaluation.

The delegations should also specify which incident conditions will be achieved prior to a transfer of command or release.

Implementing Authorities

Within his or her scope of authority, the Incident Commander establishes incident objectives, then determines strategies, resources, and ICS structure. The Incident Commander must also have the authority to establish an ICS structure adequate to protect the safety of responders and citizens, to control the spread of damage, and to protect the environment.

Management by Objectives

ICS is managed by **objectives**. Objectives are communicated throughout the entire ICS organization through the incident planning process.

Management by objectives includes:

- Establishing overarching objectives.

- Developing and issuing assignments, plans, procedures, and protocols.

- Establishing specific, measurable objectives for various incident management functional activities.

- Directing efforts to attain them, in support of defined strategic objectives.

- Documenting results to measure performance and facilitate corrective action.

Establishing and Implementing Objectives

The steps for establishing and implementing incident objectives include:

- Step 1: Understand agency policy and direction.

- Step 2: Assess incident situation.

- Step 3: Establish incident objectives.

- Step 4: Select appropriate strategy or strategies to achieve objectives.

- Step 5: Perform tactical direction.

- Step 6: Provide necessary followup.

Initial Response: Conduct a Size-Up

In an initial incident, a size-up is done to set the immediate incident objectives. The first responder to arrive must assume command and size up the situation by determining:

- Nature and magnitude of the incident

- Hazards and safety concerns

    o   Hazards facing response personnel and the public

    o   Evacuation and warnings

    o   Injuries and casualties

    o   Need to secure and isolate the area

- Initial priorities and immediate resource requirements

- Location of Incident Command Post and Staging Area

- Entrance and exit routes for responders

Overall Priorities

Throughout the incident, objectives are established based on the following priorities:

- **First Priority:** Life Safety

- **Second Priority:** Incident Stabilization

- **Third Priority:** Property Preservation

Effective Incident Objectives

For full effectiveness, incident objectives must be:

- Specific and state what's to be accomplished.

- Measurable and include a standard and timeframe.

- Attainable and reasonable.

- In accordance with the Incident Commander's authorities.

- Evaluated to determine effectiveness of strategies and tactics.

Objectives, Strategies, and Tactics

Incident Objectives, Strategies, and Tactics are three fundamental pieces of a successful incident response.

- **Incident Objectives** state what will be accomplished.

- **Strategies** establish the general plan or direction for accomplishing the incident objectives.

- **Tactics** specify how the strategies will be executed.

The Incident Commander is responsible for establishing goals and selecting strategies. The Operations Section, if it is established, is responsible for determining appropriate tactics for an incident.

Elements of an Incident Action Plan

An IAP covers an operational period and includes:

- What must be done.

- Who is responsible.

- How information will be communicated.

- What should be done if someone is injured.

The operational period is the period of time scheduled for execution of a given set of tactical actions as specified in the Incident Action Plan.

Preparedness Plans and Agreements

The Incident Commander, as well as the Command and General Staffs, should have a working knowledge of jurisdictional and agency preparedness plans and agreements.

Preparedness plans may take many forms. The most common preparedness plans are:

- Federal, State, or local Emergency Operations Plans (EOPs).

- Standard operational guidelines (SOGs).

- Standard operating procedures (SOPs).

- Jurisdictional or agency policies.

Emergency Operations Plan (EOP)

EOPs are developed at the Federal, State, and local levels to provide a uniform response to all hazards that a community may face.

EOPs written after October 2005 must be consistent with the National Incident Management System (NIMS).

Mutual-Aid Agreements

NIMS states that:

- Mutual-aid agreements are the means for one jurisdiction to provide resources, facilities, services, and other required support to another jurisdiction during an incident.

- Each jurisdiction should be party to a mutual-aid agreement with appropriate jurisdictions from which they expect to receive or to which they expect to provide assistance during an incident.

Mutual aid is the voluntary provision of resources by agencies or organizations to assist each other when existing resources are inadequate.

When combined with NIMS-oriented resource management, mutual aid allows jurisdictions to share resources among mutual-aid partners.

Mutual-Aid Agreements: All Levels

Mutual-aid agreements are used at all levels of government:

- **Local** jurisdictions participate in mutual aid through agreements with neighboring jurisdictions.

- **States** can participate in mutual aid through the Emergency Management Assistance Compact (EMAC).

- **Federal** agencies offer mutual aid to each other and to States, tribes, and territories under the NRP.

Information Derived From Plans

Plans may include information about:

- Hazards and risks in the area.

- Resources in the area.

- Other formal agreements and plans.

- Contact information for agency administrators and response personnel.

- Other pertinent information.

Lesson 4: Functional Areas & Positions

Lesson Overview

The **Functional Areas & Positions** lesson introduces you to ICS organizational components, command staff, expanding incidents, general staff, and ICS tools.

At the end of this lesson, you should be able to:

- Describe the functions of organizational positions within the Incident Command System (ICS).

- Identify the ICS tools needed to manage an incident.

- Demonstrate the use of an ICS Form 201.

This lesson provides more indepth information on ICS organizational elements.

Incident Commander

Upon arriving at an incident the higher ranking person will either assume command, maintain command as is, or reassign command to a third party.

The Incident Commander:

- Has overall incident management responsibility delegated by the appropriate jurisdictional authority.

- Develops the incident objectives to guide the incident planning process.

- Approves the Incident Action Plan and all requests pertaining to the ordering and releasing of incident resources.

In some situations or agencies, a lower ranking but more qualified person may be designated as the Incident Commander.

The Incident Commander performs **all** major ICS Command and General Staff responsibilities unless these functions are activated.

Deputy Incident Commander

The Incident Commander may have one or more Deputies. Deputies may be assigned at the Incident Command, Section, or Branch levels. The only ICS requirement regarding the use of a Deputy is that the Deputy must be fully qualified and equally capable to assume the position.

The three primary reasons to designate a Deputy Incident Commander are to:

- Perform specific tasks as requested by the Incident Commander.

- Perform the incident command function in a relief capacity (e.g., to take over the next operational period). In this case the Deputy will assume the primary role.

- Represent an Assisting Agency that may share jurisdiction or have jurisdiction in the future.

Command Staff

The Command Staff is only activated in response to the needs of the incident. Command Staff includes the following positions:

- Public Information Officer

- Liaison Officer

- Safety Officer

Command Staff carry out staff functions needed to support the Incident Commander. These functions include interagency liaison, incident safety, and public information. The following Command Staff positions are established to assign responsibility for key activities not specifically identified in the General Staff functional elements.

Command Staff	Responsibilities
Public Information Officer (PIO)	The PIO is responsible for interfacing with the public and media and/or with other agencies with incident-related information requirements. The PIO develops accurate and complete information on the incident's cause, size, and current situation; resources committed; and other matters of general interest for both internal and external consumption. The PIO may also perform a key public information-monitoring role.
	Only one incident PIO should be designated. Assistants may be assigned from other agencies or departments involved. The Incident Commander must approve the release of all incident-related information.
Safety Officer (SO)	The SO monitors incident operations and advises the Incident Commander on all matters relating to operational safety, including the health and safety of emergency responder personnel. The ultimate responsibility for the safe conduct of incident

	management operations rests with the Incident Commander or Unified Command and supervisors at all levels of incident management. The SO is, in turn, responsible to the Incident Commander for the set of systems and procedures necessary to ensure ongoing assessment of hazardous environments, coordination of multiagency safety efforts, and implementation of measures to promote emergency responder safety, as well as the general safety of incident operations. The SO has emergency authority to stop and/or prevent unsafe acts during incident operations. In a Unified Command structure, a single SO should be designated, in spite of the fact that multiple jurisdictions and/or functional agencies may be involved. The SO must also ensure the coordination of safety management functions and issues across jurisdictions, across functional agencies, and with private-sector and nongovernmental organizations.
Liaison Officer (LNO)	The LNO is the point of contact for representatives of other governmental agencies, nongovernmental organizations, and/or private entities. In either a single or Unified Command structure, representatives from assisting or cooperating agencies and organizations coordinate through the LNO. Agency and/or organizational representatives assigned to an incident must have the authority to speak for their parent agencies and/or organizations on all matters, following appropriate consultations with their agency leadership. Assistants and personnel from other agencies or organizations (public or private) involved in incident management activities may be assigned to the LNO to facilitate coordination.

Source: National Incident Management System (NIMS)

Agency Representative

An Agency Representative is an individual assigned to an incident from an assisting or cooperating agency. The Agency Representative is delegated authority to make decisions on matters affecting that agency's participation at the incident.

Assisting Agency

An agency or jurisdiction will often send resources to assist at an incident. In ICS these are called Assisting Agencies.

An Assisting Agency is defined as an agency or organization providing personnel, services, or other resources to the agency with **direct responsibility for incident management.**

Cooperating Agency

A Cooperating Agency is an agency **supplying assistance other than direct operational or support functions** or resources to the incident management effort.

Don't get confused between an Assisting Agency and a Cooperating Agency! An Assisting Agency has direct responsibility for incident response, whereas a Cooperating Agency is simply offering assistance.

Assistants

In a large or complex incident, Command Staff members may need one or more Assistants to help manage their workloads. Each Command Staff member is responsible for organizing his or her Assistants for maximum efficiency. Assistants are subordinates of principle Command Staff positions.

As the title indicates, Assistants should have a level of technical capability, qualifications, and responsibility subordinate to the primary positions.

Assistants may also be assigned to Unit Leaders (e.g., at camps to supervise unit activities).

Expanding Incidents

An incident may start small and then expand. As the incident grows in scope and the number of resources needed increases, there may be a need to activate Teams, Divisions, Groups, Branches, or Sections to maintain an appropriate span of control.

The ability to delegate the supervision of resources not only frees up the Incident Commander to perform critical decisionmaking and evaluation duties, but also clearly defines the lines of communication to everyone involved in the incident.

Operations Section

The Operations Section:

- Directs and coordinates all incident tactical operations.

- Is typically one of the first organizations to be assigned to the incident.

- Expands from the bottom up.

- Has the most incident resources.

- May have Staging Areas and special organizations.

Operations Section Chief

The Operations Section Chief:

- Is responsible to the Incident Commander for the direct management of all incident-related operational activities.

- Establishes tactical objectives for each operational period.

- Has direct involvement in the preparation of the Incident Action Plan.

The Operations Section Chief may have one or more Deputies assigned. The assignment of Deputies from other agencies may be advantageous in the case of multijurisdictional incidents.

Operations Section: Staging Areas

Staging Areas are set up at the incident where resources can wait for a tactical assignment.

All resources in the Staging Area are assigned and ready for deployment. Out-of-service resources are NOT located at the Staging Area.

Staging Areas: Chain of Command

After a Staging Area has been designated and named, a Staging Area Manager will be assigned. The Staging Area Manager will report to the Operations Section Chief or to the Incident Commander if the Operations Section Chief has not been designated.

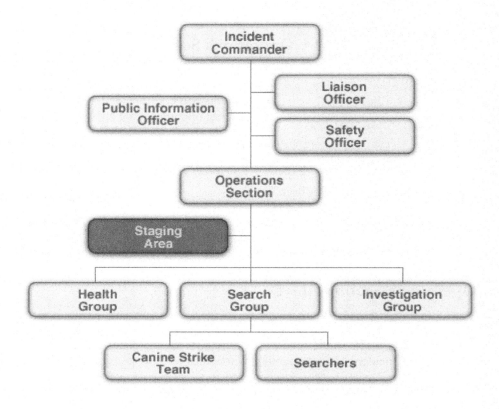

Divisions and Groups

Divisions are established to divide an incident into physical or geographical areas of operation.

Groups are established to divide the incident into functional areas of operation.

Branches

Branches may be used to serve several purposes, and may be functional or geographic in nature. Branches are established when the number of Divisions or Groups exceeds the recommended span of control of one supervisor to three to seven subordinates for the Operations Section Chief. Branches are identified by Roman numerals or functional name, and are managed by a Branch Director.

Air Operations Branch

Some incidents may require the use of aviation resources to provide tactical or logistical support. On smaller incidents, aviation resources will be limited in number and will report directly to the Incident Commander or to the Operations Section Chief.

On larger incidents, it may be desirable to activate a separate Air Operations organization to coordinate the use of aviation resources. The Air Operations organization will then be established at the Branch level, reporting directly to the Operations Section Chief.

The Air Operations Branch Director can establish two functional groups. The Air Tactical Group coordinates all airborne activity. The Air Support Group provides all incident ground-based support to aviation resources.

Planning Section

The Planning Section has responsibility for:

- Maintaining resource status.

- Maintaining and displaying situation status.

- Preparing the Incident Action Plan (IAP).

- Assisting or developing alternative strategies

- Providing documentation services.

- Preparing the Demobilization Plan.

- Providing a primary location for Technical Specialists assigned to an incident.

One of the most important functions of the Planning Section is to look beyond the current and next operational period and anticipate potential problems or events.

Information and Intelligence

The Planning Section is typically responsible for gathering and disseminating information and intelligence critical to the incident. Based on the incident needs, the Information and Intelligence function may be activated as a fifth General Staff section, as an element within the Operations or Planning Sections, or as part of the Command Staff.

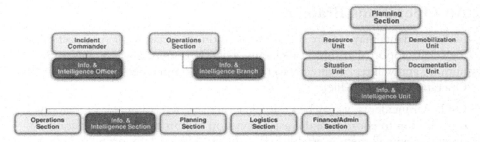

The analysis and sharing of information and intelligence are important elements of ICS.

In this context, intelligence includes not only national security or other types of classified information but also other operational information, such as risk assessments, medical intelligence (i.e., surveillance), weather information, geospatial data, structural designs, toxic contaminant levels, and utilities and public works data, that may come from a variety of different sources.

Traditionally, information and intelligence functions are located in the Planning Section.

However, in exceptional situations, the Incident Commander may need to assign the information and intelligence functions to other parts of the ICS organization. In any case, information and intelligence must be appropriately analyzed and shared with personnel, designated by the Incident Commander, who have proper clearance and a "need-to-know" to ensure that they support decisionmaking.

The information and intelligence function may be organized in one of the following ways:

- **Within the Command Staff.** This option may be most appropriate in incidents with little need for tactical or classified intelligence and in which incident-related intelligence is provided by supporting Agency Representatives, through real-time reach-back capabilities.

- **As a Unit Within the Planning Section.** This option may be most appropriate in an incident with some need for tactical intelligence and when no law enforcement entity is a member of the Unified Command.

- **As a Branch Within the Operations Section.** This option may be most appropriate in incidents with a high need for tactical intelligence (particularly classified intelligence) and when law enforcement is a member of the Unified Command.

- **As a Separate General Staff Section.** This option may be most appropriate when an incident is heavily influenced by intelligence factors or when there is a need to manage and/or analyze a large

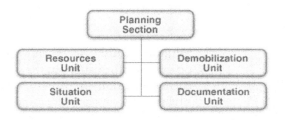

volume of classified or highly sensitive intelligence or information. This option is particularly relevant to a terrorism incident, for which intelligence plays a crucial role throughout the incident life cycle.

Regardless of how it is organized, the information and intelligence function is also responsible for developing, conducting, and managing information-related security plans and operations as directed by the Incident Action Plan.

These can include information security and operational security activities, as well as the complex task of ensuring that sensitive information of all types (e.g., classified information, sensitive law enforcement information, proprietary and personal information, or export-controlled information) is handled in a way that not only safeguards the information but also ensures that it gets to those who need access to it so that they can effectively and safely conduct their missions.

The information and intelligence function also has the responsibility for coordinating information- and operational-security matters with public awareness activities that fall under the responsibility of the Public Information Officer, particularly where such public awareness activities may affect information or operations security.

Planning Section Key Personnel

The Planning Section will have a Planning Section Chief. The Planning Section Chief may have a Deputy.

Technical Specialists are advisors with special skills required at the incident. Technical Specialists will initially report to the Planning Section, work within that Section, or be reassigned to another part of the organization. Technical Specialists can be in any discipline required (e.g., aviation, environment, hazardous materials, training, human resources, etc.).

Planning Section Units

The major responsibilities of Planning Units are:

- **Resources Unit:** Responsible for all check-in activity and for maintaining the status on all personnel and equipment resources assigned to the incident.

-

-

- **Situation Unit:** Collects and processes information on the current situation, prepares situation displays and situation summaries, develops maps and projections.

- **Documentation Unit:** Prepares the Incident Action Plan, maintains all incident-related documentation, and provides duplication services.

- **Demobilization Unit:** On large, complex incidents, the Demobilization Unit will assist in ensuring that an orderly, safe, and cost-effective movement of personnel is made when they are no longer required at the incident.

Logistics Section

Early recognition of the need for a Logistics Section can reduce time and money spent on an incident. The Logistics Section is responsible for all support requirements, including:

- Communications

- Medical support to incident personnel

- Food for incident personnel

- Supplies, facilities, and ground support

It is important to remember that Logistics Unit functions, except for the Supply Unit, are geared to **supporting personnel and resources directly assigned to the incident**.

Logistics Section: Service Branch

The Service Branch may be made up of the following units:

- The **Communications Unit** is responsible for developing plans for the effective use of incident communications equipment and facilities, installing and testing of communications equipment, supervision of the Incident Communications Center, distribution of communications equipment to incident personnel, and the maintenance and repair of communications equipment.

- The **Medical Unit** is responsible for the development of the Medical Plan, obtaining medical aid and transportation for injured and ill incident personnel, and preparation of reports and records.

- The **Food Unit** is responsible for supplying the food needs for the entire incident, including all remote locations (e.g., Camps, Staging Areas), as well as providing food for personnel unable to leave tactical field assignments.

Logistics Section: Support Branch

The Support Branch within the Logistics Section may include the following units:

- The **Supply Unit** is responsible for ordering personnel, equipment, and supplies; receiving and storing all supplies for the incident; maintaining an inventory of supplies; and servicing nonexpendable supplies and equipment.

- The **Facilities Unit** is responsible for the layout and activation of incident facilities (e.g., Base, Camp(s), and Incident Command Post (ICP)). The Facilities Unit Leader provides sleeping and sanitation facilities for incident personnel and manages Base and Camp(s) operations. Each facility (Base, Camp) is assigned a manager who reports to the Facilities Unit Leader and is responsible for managing the operation of the facility. The basic functions or activities of the Base and Camp Managers are to provide security service and general maintenance.

- The **Ground Support Unit** is responsible for supporting out-of-service resources; transporting personnel, supplies, food, and equipment; fueling, service, maintenance, and repair of vehicles and other ground support equipment; and implementing the Traffic Plan for the incident.

Finance/Administration Section

The Finance/Administration Section:

- Is established when incident management activities require finance and other administrative support services.

-

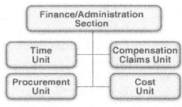

- Handles claims related to property damage, injuries, or fatalities at the incident.

Not all incidents will require a separate Finance/Administration Section. If only one specific function is needed (e.g., cost analysis), a Technical Specialist assigned to the Planning Section could provide these services.

Finance/Administration Units

Finance/Administration Units include the following:

- The **Time Unit** is responsible for equipment and personnel time recording.

- The **Procurement Unit** is responsible for administering all financial matters pertaining to vendor contracts, leases, and fiscal agreements.

- The **Compensation/Claims Unit** is responsible for financial concerns resulting from property damage, injuries, or fatalities at the incident.

- The **Cost Unit** is responsible for tracking costs, analyzing cost data, making cost estimates, and recommending cost-saving measures.

ICS Tools

Some important tools you should have available at the incident include:

- ICS Forms

- Position Description and Responsibilities Document

- Emergency Operations Plan

- Agency Policies and Procedures Manual

- Maps

ICS Forms

When receiving ICS forms, some questions you should ask yourself about each form are:

- **Purpose** — What function does the form perform?

- **Preparation** — Who is responsible for preparing the form?

- **Distribution** — Who needs to receive this information?

ICS Form 201, Incident Briefing

The Incident Briefing Form (ICS Form 201) is an eight-part form that provides an Incident Command/Unified Command with status information that can be used for briefing incoming resources, an incoming Incident Commander or team, or an immediate supervisor. The basic information includes:

- Incident situation (map, significant events)

- Incident objectives

- Summary of current actions

- Status of resources assigned or ordered for the incident or event

Occasionally, the ICS Form 201 serves as the initial Incident Action Plan (IAP) until a Planning Section has been established and generates, at the direction of the Incident Commander, an IAP.

The ICS Form 201 is also suitable for briefing individuals newly assigned to the Command and General Staff.

Completing the ICS Form 201

The following demonstrates how to complete the Incident Briefing ICS Form 201 for a hostage incident.

In Block 1, print a unique incident name. In **Block 2**, print the date the form was prepared in a month, day, year format. In **Block 3**, enter the time the form was prepared using a 24-hour clock. The person preparing this page signs in **Block 5**.

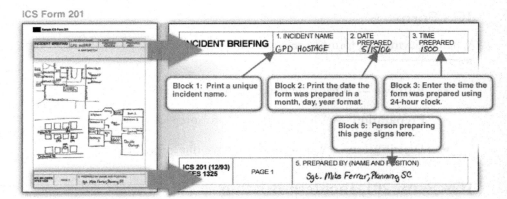

In **Block 4** develop a map sketch that shows the incident perimeter and control lines, resource assignments, and incident facilities, along with other special information on a sketch map or attached to the topographic map.

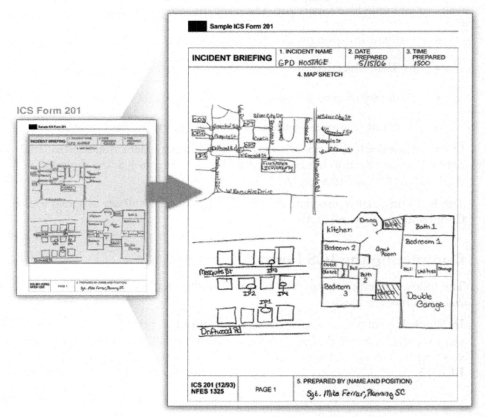

In **Block 6** is the current status of strategy/tactics, initial objectives, and history. The person preparing this page signs it at the bottom.

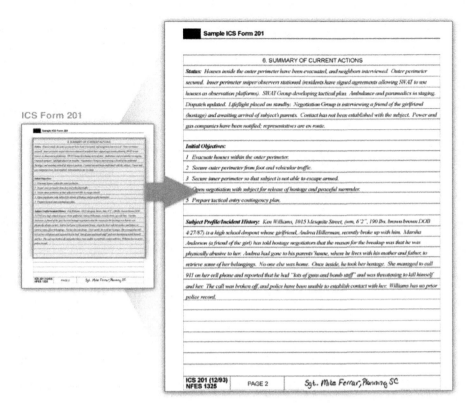

ICS Form 201

In **Block 7** is the current organizational chart. Enter the names of the individuals assigned to each position on the organization chart. The person preparing this page signs it at the bottom.enter information about the resources allocated to the incident.

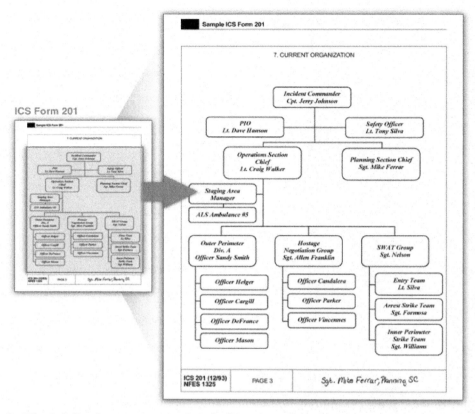

In **Block 8** list the resources ordered, a resource identification code (with a 3-letter code if available), the estimated time of arrival or an X if already in place, and the location where the resource will be assigned. The person preparing this page signs it at the bottom.

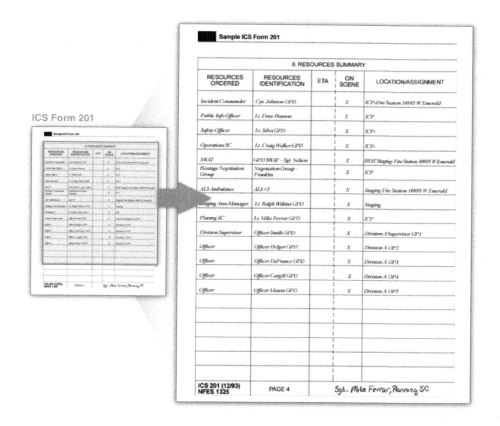

ICS Form 201

Other Commonly Used ICS Forms

Form Number	Title	Who Completes
Form 201	Incident Briefing	Section Chief
Form 202	Response Objectives	Section Chief
Form 203	Organization Assignment List	Resources Unit
Form 204	Assignment List	Section Chief, Staff
Form 205	Incident Radio Communications Plan	Communications Unit
Form 206	Medical Plan	Medical Unit
Form 208	Site Safety and Control Plan	Safety Officer, Staff
Form 209	Incident Status Summary	Resources Unit

Form 210	Status Change Card	Staff
Form 211	Check-In List	Staff
Form 213	General Message	Staff
Form 214	Unit Log	Staff
Form 215	Operational Planning Worksheet	Staff
Form 215a	Incident Action Plan Safety Analysis	Safety Officer, Staff
Form 220	Air Operations Summary Worksheet	Air Operations Unit
Form 221	Demobilization Checkout	Resources Unit

Lesson 5: Briefings

Lesson Overview

The **Briefings** lesson introduces you to different types of briefings and meetings.

At the end of this lesson you should be able to:

- Describe components of field, staff, and section briefings/meetings.

- Plan to give an operational period briefing.

Effective Meetings and Briefings

Effective briefings and meetings are:

- An essential element to good supervision and incident management.

- Intended to pass along vital information required in the completion incident response actions.

Typically, these briefings are concise and do not include long discussions or complex decisionmaking. Rather, they allow incident managers and supervisors to communicate specific information and expectations for the upcoming work period and to answer questions.

Levels of Briefings

There are three types of briefings/meetings used in ICS: staff level, field level, and section level.

- **Staff-level briefings** are delivered to resources assigned to nonoperational and support tasks at the Incident Command Post or Base.

- **Field-level briefings** are delivered to individual resources or crews who are assigned to operational tasks and/or work at or near the incident site.

- **Section-level briefings** are delivered to an entire Section and include the Operational Period Briefing.

Briefing Type	Description
Staff-	This level typically involves resources assigned to

Level Briefings	nonoperational and support tasks that are commonly performed at the Incident Base or Command Post. These briefings will be delivered to individual staff members or full units within a section. These briefings occur at the beginning of the assignment to the incident and as necessary during the assignment.
	The supervisor attempts to clarify tasks and scope of the work as well as define reporting schedule, subordinate responsibilities and delegated authority, and the supervisor's expectations. The supervisor will also introduce coworkers and define actual workspace, sources of work supplies, and work schedule.
Field-Level Briefings	This level typically involves resources assigned to operational tasks and/or work at or near the incident site. These briefings will be delivered to individual subordinates, full crews, or multiple crews such as Strike Teams or Task Forces and will occur at the beginning of an operational shift.
	The location will usually be near the work site or just prior to mobilization to the field. The supervisor attempts to focus the subordinates on their specific tasks and helps define work area, reporting relationships, and expectations.
Section-Level Briefings	This level typically involves the briefing of an entire Section (Operations, Planning, Logistics, or Finance/Administration) and is done by the specific Section Chief. These briefings occur at the beginning of the assignment to the incident and after the arrival of Section supervisory staff. The Section Chief may schedule periodic briefings at specific times (once per day) or when necessary. A unique briefing in this category is the **Operational Period Briefing** (also called a Shift Operations Briefing). Here, the Operations Section Chief presents the plan for all operational elements for the specific operational period. This specific briefing is done at the beginning of each operation shift and prior to the operational resources being deployed to the area of work. Often, a field-level briefing will take place subsequent to the completion of the Operational Period Briefing.
	During any section-level briefing, the supervisor attempts to share incident-wide direction from the Incident Commander (IC), how the direction impacts the Section staff, and specific ways the Section will support the IC's direction. The supervisor will establish Section staffing requirements, Section

	work tasks, Section-wide scheduling rules, and overall timelines for meetings and completion of work products.

Briefing Topics Checklist

Below is a list of topics that you may want to include in a briefing.

- Current Situation and Objectives

- Safety Issues and Emergency Procedures

- Work Tasks

- Facilities and Work Areas

- Communications Protocols

- Supervisory/Performance Expectations

- Process for Acquiring Resources, Supplies, and Equipment

- Work Schedules

- Questions or Concerns

Operational Period Briefing

The Operational Period Briefing:

- Is conducted at the beginning of each operational period.

- Presents the Incident Action Plan for the upcoming period to supervisory personnel within the Operations Section.

- Should be concise.

In addition to the Operations Section Chief, the other members of the Command and General Staffs as well as specific support elements (i.e., Communications Unit, Medical Unit) can provide important information needed for safe and effective performance during the shift.

Operational Period Briefing: Agenda

The Operational Period Briefing is facilitated by the Planning Section Chief and follows a set agenda. A typical briefing includes the following:

- The **Planning Section Chief** reviews the agenda and facilitates the briefing.

- The **Incident Commander** presents incident objectives or confirms existing objectives.
  Note: Objectives may be presented by the Planning Section Chief.

- The **Current Operations Section Chief** provides current assessment and accomplishments.

- The **on-coming Operations Section Chief** covers the work assignments and staffing of divisions and groups for the upcoming operational period.

- **Technical Specialists** present updates on conditions affecting the response (weather, fire behavior, environmental factors).

- The **Safety Officer** reviews specific risks to operational resources and the identified safety/mitigation measures.

- The **Special Operations Chief** briefs on areas such as Air Operations (if activated).

- **Specific Section Chief/Unit Leaders** present information related to ensuring safe and efficient operations.

- The **Incident Commander** reiterates his or her operational concerns and directs resources to deploy.

- The **Planning Section Chief** announces the next planning meeting and Operational Period Briefing, then adjourns the meeting.

Lesson 6: Organizational Flexibility

Lesson Overview

The **Organizational Flexibility** lesson introduces you to flexibility within the standard ICS organizational structure and the ICS organization's principle of management by objectives.

At the end of this lesson you should be able to:

- Explain how the modular organization expands and contracts.

- Given a scenario, complete a complexity analysis.

- Define the five types of incidents.

Flexibility and Standardization

A key principle of ICS is its **flexibility**. The ICS organization may be expanded easily from a very small size for routine operations to a larger organization capable of handling catastrophic events.

Standardization within ICS does NOT limit flexibility. ICS works for small, routine operations as well as catastrophic events.

Flexibility does NOT mean that the ICS feature of common terminology is superceded. Flexibility is allowed only within the standard ICS organizational structure and position titles.

Modular Organization

Incident command organizational structure is based on:

- Size and complexity of the incident.

- Specifics of the hazard environment created by the incident.

- Incident planning process and incident objectives.

ICS Expansion and Contraction

Although there are no hard-and-fast rules, it is important to remember that:

- Only functions and positions that are necessary to achieve incident objectives are filled.

- Each activated element must have a person in charge.

- An effective span of control .must be maintained.

Activation of Organizational Elements

Many incidents will never require the activation of the entire Command or General Staff or entire list of organizational elements within each Section. Other incidents will require some or all members of the Command Staff and all sub-elements of each General Staff Section.

The decision to activate an element (Section, Branch, Unit, Division, or Group) must be based on incident objectives and resource needs.

An important concept is that many organizational elements may be activated in various sections **without** activating the Section Chief.

For example, the Situation Unit can be activated without a Planning Section Chief assigned. In this case, the supervision of the Situation Unit will rest with the Incident Commander.

Avoid Combining Positions

It is tempting to combine ICS positions to gain staffing efficiency. Rather than combining positions, you may assign the same individual to supervise multiple units.

When assigning personnel to multiple positions, do **not** use nonstandard titles. Creating new titles may be unrecognizable to assisting or cooperating personnel and may cause confusion.

Resource Management

Maintaining an accurate and up-to-date picture of resource utilization is a critical component of incident management. The incident resource management process consists of the following:

- Establishment of resource needs (kind/type/quantity)

- Resource ordering (actually getting what you need)

- Check-in process and tracking (knowing what resources you have and where they are)

- Resource utilization and evaluation (using the resources effectively)

- Resource demobilization (releasing resources that are no longer needed)

Anticipating Incident Resource Needs

Experience and training will help you to predict workloads and corresponding staffing needs. As the graphic below illustrates, an incident may build faster than resources can arrive. Eventually, a sufficient number of resources arrive and begin to control the incident. As the incident declines, resources then exceed incident needs.

Predicting Incident Workload

Incident workload patterns are often predictable throughout the incident life cycle. Several examples are provided below:

- **Operations Section:** The workload on Operations is immediate and often massive. On a rapidly escalating incident, the Operations Section Chief must determine appropriate tactics; organize, assign, and supervise resources; and at the same time participate in the planning process.

- **Planning Section:** The Resources and Situation Units will be very busy in the initial phases of the incident. In the later stages, the Documentation and Demobilization Units workload will increase.

- **Logistics Section:** The Supply and Communications Units will be very active in the initial and final stages of the incident.

Analyzing Incident Complexity

It is important to strike the right balance when determining resource needs. Having too few resources can lead to loss of life and property, while having too many resources can result in unqualified personnel deployed without proper supervision. A **complexity analysis** can help:

- Identify resource requirements.

- Determine if the existing management structure is appropriate.

Incident Complexity and Resource Needs

When incident complexity increases, your resource needs and ICS structure grow accordingly.

Resource Kinds and Types

To ensure that responders get the right personnel and equipment, ICS resources are categorized by:

- **Kinds of Resources**: Describe what the resource is (for example: medic, firefighter, Planning Section Chief, helicopters, ambulances, combustible gas indicators, bulldozers).

- **Types of Resources**: Describe the size, capability, and staffing qualifications of a specific kind of resource.

Importance of Resource Typing

Requesting a resource kind without specifying a resource type could result in an inadequate resource arriving on the scene.

The Order: "We need a HazMat team."

What You Needed   What Arrived

Resource Typing

Resource types range from Type 1 (most capable) to Type 4 (least capable), letting you reserve the appropriate level of resource for your incident by describing the size, capability, and staffing qualifications of a specific resource.

Resource Typing and NIMS

Resource typing is a key component of the NIMS. This effort assists all Federal, State, territory, tribal, and local jurisdictions locate, request, and track resources to assist neighboring jurisdictions when local capability is overwhelmed.

The National Integration Center encourages Federal, State, territory, and local officials to use the 120 NIMS Resource Typing Definitions as they develop or update response assets inventories.

Additional Resource Terminology

As covered in ICS-100, the following terms apply to resources:

- **Task Forces** are a **combination of mixed resources** with common communications operating under the direct supervision of a Task Force Leader.

- **Strike Teams** are a set number of resources **of the same kind and type** with common communications operating under the direct supervision of a Strike Team Leader.

- **Single Resource:** An individual, a piece of equipment and its personnel complement, or a crew or team of individuals with an identified work supervisor that can be used on an incident.

Incident Typing: Overview

Incidents, like resources, may be categorized into five types based on complexity. **Type 5 incidents are the least complex** and **Type 1 the most complex.**

Incident typing may be used to:

- Make decisions about resource requirements.

- Order Incident Management Teams (IMTs). An IMT is made up of the Command and General Staff members in an ICS organization.

The incident type corresponds to both the number of resources required and the anticipated incident duration.

Type 5 Incident

Characteristics of a Type 5 Incident are as follows:

- **Resources:** One or two single resources with up to six personnel. Command and General Staff positions (other than the Incident Commander) are not activated.

- **Time Span:** Incident is contained within the first operational period and often within a few hours after resources arrive on scene. No written Incident Action Plan is required.

Examples include a vehicle fire, an injured person, or a police traffic stop.

Type 4 Incident

Characteristics of a Type 4 Incident are as follows:

- **Resources:** Command Staff and General Staff functions are activated (only if needed). Several single resources are required to mitigate the incident.

- **Time Span:** Limited to one operational period in the control phase. No written Incident Action Plan is required for non-HazMat incidents. A documented operational briefing is completed.

Type 3 Incident

Characteristics of a Type 3 Incident are as follows:

- **Resources:** When capabilities exceed initial attack, the appropriate ICS positions should be added to match the complexity of the incident. Some or all of the Command and General Staff positions may be activated, as well as Division or Group Supervisor and/or Unit Leader level positions. An Incident Management Team (IMT) or incident command organization manages initial action incidents with a significant number of resources, and an extended attack incident until containment/control is achieved.

- **Time Span:** The incident may extend into multiple operational periods and a written Incident Action Plan may be required for each operational period.

Type 2 Incident

Characteristics of a Type 2 Incident are as follows:

- **Resources:** Regional and/or national resources are required to safely and effectively manage the operations. Most or all Command and General Staff positions are filled. Operations personnel typically do not exceed 200 per operational period and the total does not exceed 500. The agency administrator/official is responsible for the incident complexity analysis, agency administrator briefings, and written delegation of authority.

- **Time Span:** The incident is expected to go into multiple operational periods. A written Incident Action Plan is required for each operational period.

Type 1 Incident

Characteristics of a Type 1 Incident are as follows:

- **Resources:** National resources are required to safely and effectively manage the operations. All Command and General Staff positions are activated, and Branches need to be established. Operations personnel often exceed 500 per operational period and total personnel will usually exceed 1,000. There is a high impact on the local jurisdiction, requiring additional staff for office administrative and support functions. The incident may result in a disaster declaration.

- **Time Span:** The incident is expected to go into multiple operational periods. A written Incident Action Plan is required for each operational period.

Incident Management Teams (IMTs)

An Incident Management Team (IMT) may be used to respond to an incident. IMTs include Command and General Staff members. IMT types correspond to incident type and include:

- Type 5: Local Village and Township Level

- Type 4: City, County, or Fire District Level

- Type 3: State or Metropolitan Area Level

- Type 2: National and State Level

- Type 1: National and State Level (Type 1 Incident)

Team members are certified as having the necessary training and experience to fulfill IMT positions.

Lesson 7: Transfer of Command

Lesson Overview

The **Transfer of Command** lesson introduces you to transfer of command briefings and procedures.

At the end of this lesson, you should be able to:

- Describe the process of transfer of command.

- List the essential elements of information involved in transfer of command.

Transfer of Command

Transfer of command is **the process of moving the responsibility for incident command from one Incident Commander to another.**

When Command Is Transferred

Transfer of command may take place for many reasons, including when:

- A jurisdiction or agency is legally required to take command.

- Change of command is necessary for effectiveness or efficiency.

- Incident complexity changes.

- There is a need to relieve personnel on incidents of extended duration.

- Personal emergencies (e.g., Incident Commander has a family emergency).

- Agency administrator directs a change in command.

A More Qualified Person Arrives

The arrival of a more qualified person does NOT necessarily mean a change in incident command. .The more qualified individual may:

- Assume command according to agency guidelines.

- Maintain command as it is and monitor command activity and effectiveness.

- Request a more qualified Incident Commander from the agency with a higher level of jurisdictional responsibility.

Transfer of Command Procedures

One of the main features of ICS is a procedure to transfer command with minimal disruption to the incident. This procedure may be used any time personnel in supervisory positions change.

Whenever possible, transfer of command should:

- Take place face-to-face.

- Include a complete briefing.

The effective time and date of the transfer should be communicated to personnel.

Transfer of Command Briefing Elements

A transfer of command briefing should always take place. The briefing should include:

- Situation status.

- Incident objectives and priorities.

- Current organization.

- Resource assignments.

- Resources ordered and en route.

- Incident facilities.

- Incident communications plan.

- Incident prognosis, concerns, and other issues.

- Introduction of Command and General Staff members.

Incident Briefing Form (ICS Form 201)

Agency policies and incident specific issues may alter the transfer of command process. In all cases, the information shared must be documented and saved for easy retrieval during and after the incident.

The initial Incident Commander can use the ICS Form 201 to document actions and situational information.

For more complex transfer of command situations, every aspect of the incident must be documented and included in the transfer of command briefing.

CPSIA information can be obtained
at www.ICGtesting.com
Printed in the USA
LVOW13s0045131017

552272LV00020B/630/P